The Person I Became
So Can You!

Asri Byll DNP, RN, CMSRN

The Person I Became
Copyright © 2024 by Asri Byll, DNP, RN, CMSRN
All rights reserved.

No part of this book may be reproduced, distributed, or transmitted in any form or by any means without the publisher's prior written permission except as permitted by U.S. copyright law.

Published by [Self-Published on Amazon KDP]
ISBN: [M0D2078523440]

This is a memoir. The events and experiences in this book reflect the author's personal life and journey. Some names and identifying details have been changed to protect individuals' privacy.

Fiverr Cover design by M A Rehman @rehmanx_x
Fiverr Editing by Britney Mason @britney_mason

For more information, contact: asribyll@yahoo.com or visit social media pages **@nurse_byll**

Printed in the United States of America.

The Person I Became

Acknowledgments

Writing this memoir has been a deeply personal and transformative journey that I could not have undertaken alone. There are many people to whom I owe a debt of gratitude for their support, encouragement, and inspiration throughout this process.

First and foremost, I want to express my deepest thanks to my family, who have always supported me in every endeavor. To my wife, who has been my lifelong companion, sharing in both my joys and my struggles, unconditional love and belief in me have been my anchor and my motivation. To my kids, I love you.

I am grateful to my friends, especially members of the Brothers Abroad group who have walked with me through the ups and downs of life. Your companionship, wisdom, and humor have enriched my life in countless ways. Thank you for the deep conversations, shared experiences, and moments of laughter that have shaped the person I am today. You have been my sounding boards, mirrors, and guides, and I am forever thankful for your presence in my life.

To my mentors and teachers, thank you for challenging, guiding, and encouraging me to think deeply and critically. Your wisdom and insight have been invaluable in shaping my perspective and understanding of the world. I am especially grateful to those who encouraged me to embrace my vulnerabilities and to write with honesty and courage. Your belief in my ability to tell my story has been a driving force in completing this memoir.

I also wish to acknowledge the many individuals whose stories and experiences have touched my life and influenced the content of this memoir. Whether through brief encounters or long-lasting relationships, your perspectives have broadened my understanding and enriched my journey. Thank you for sharing your experiences with me and for allowing me to see the world through your eyes.

Finally, to the readers of this memoir: thank you for taking the time to journey with me through these pages. I hope my experiences, reflections, and insights resonate with you in some way and inspire you to embrace your own experiences, emotions, and viewpoints with an open heart. I wrote this book for you, and I am grateful for your willingness to share in my story.

This memoir is a testament to the many people who have shaped my life, and I am deeply thankful for each and every one of you.

Dedication

To my life partner Paula and my kids Skylar, Eli, Madalise, and Gabrielle, I love you all. I also want to thank Seth and Dzigbordi Ahiekpor for their guidance through my initial settlement in the USA.

This memoir is for you and anyone who dares to embrace life with an open heart, a curious mind, and a courageous spirit.

May we all continue to grow, learn, and connect as we navigate this beautiful tapestry of experiences, emotions, and viewpoints together.

The Person I Became

Table of Content

The Person I Became 1

Acknowledgments 3

Dedication 5

Introduction: 7

A Journey of Discovery and Empowerment 7

Chapter 1: 10

Defining the Journey 10

Chapter 2: 21

Balancing Act 21

Chapter 3: 35

Lessons Learned 35

Chapter 4: 48

Guided by Mentorship 48

Chapter 5: 60

From Struggles to Success 60

Chapter 6: 70

The Power of Voice and Influence 70

Chapter 7: 83

Embrace Experiences, Emotions, and Viewpoints 83

Conclusion: 97

Embrace Your Journey 97

    Appendix: 100

    Resources for Continued Growth 100

Summary 104

Introduction: A Journey of Discovery and Empowerment

Welcome, dear reader, to *The Person I Became*. Within these pages lies a journey—one of self-discovery, resilience, and empowerment. As you embark on this literary adventure with me, I invite you to open your heart and mind to the transformative power of personal growth and authenticity. My story begins with a simple yet profound inspiration: a desire to leave a lasting legacy for my loved ones and empower them with openness and authenticity. This journey spans years of triumphs and challenges, moments of clarity and uncertainty, but above all, it is a journey of becoming—the person I was always meant to be, and the person I am today.

Each chapter of this book stands as a testament to the resilience of the human spirit—a celebration of the highs and lows that shape our lives and a reminder that within every obstacle lies an opportunity for growth. From humble beginnings to moments of success, my journey is a tapestry woven with threads of perseverance, determination, and unwavering belief in the power of possibility.

In these pages, you will accompany me as I navigate the complexities of balancing work, education, and family responsibilities. You will witness the struggles and triumphs of overcoming financial obstacles and pursuing dreams with steadfast conviction. Through this journey, you will gain insight into the transformative power of resilience, adaptability, and maintaining a positive outlook in the face of adversity.

But this is not just my story—it is also a story of mentorship, guidance, and the profound impact of human connection. Throughout my journey, I have been blessed with mentors who believed in me, encouraged me, and helped me unlock my full potential. Now, I am committed to paying it forward by guiding and supporting others on their own paths of growth and empowerment.

At its core, *The Person I Became* is a testament to the transformative power of authenticity—the courage to embrace our true selves, the strength to speak our truth, and the resilience to navigate life's challenges with grace and dignity. It serves as a reminder that within each of us lies the power to create the life we desire, to overcome obstacles, and to leave a lasting legacy for future generations.

So, dear reader, I invite you to journey with me through the pages of *The Person I Became*. May this book inspire and empower you, reminding you that within every challenge lies an opportunity for growth and within every heart lies the power to change the world. As my boss always says, "Trust the process" (SMJ)—the learning is in the journey.

Chapter 1:
Defining the Journey

The journey of self-discovery is not a straight path but a winding road filled with unexpected twists and turns. It begins with a spark—a moment of inspiration, a desire for change, a longing for something more. For me, this journey started with a simple yet profound realization: a desire to leave a legacy for my loved ones and to empower them with authenticity and openness.

As I reflect on the milestones and challenges that have shaped my path, I am reminded of the pivotal moments that have defined who I am today. From humble beginnings to profound successes, each step along the way has been guided by a deep sense of purpose and a commitment to personal growth.

One of the earliest milestones in my journey was the decision to pursue a career in nursing. This choice was driven by a deep-seated belief in the power of compassion and empathy to heal and uplift others—a calling that stirred within me. My conviction was further solidified during my time working in an acute care hospital, first as a food service worker and later as an emergency room clerk.

The Person I Became

Witnessing firsthand the dedication and care of healthcare professionals ignited my passion to join that impactful field. Navigating through nursing school was undoubtedly challenging, but quitting was never an option. Long hours of studying, countless exams, and moments of doubt tested my resolve, but I persevered. Graduating from nursing school marked a significant milestone in my life, a testament to my determination and commitment to my chosen path.

Since becoming a nurse, my life has been profoundly transformed. Beyond acquiring clinical skills and knowledge, this journey has been one of personal growth and a deeper appreciation for the fragility and resilience of life. Each day offers a chance to make a difference—providing comfort and support to those in need and advocating for their well-being.

One of the most rewarding aspects of my role is the privilege of receiving phone calls from friends and family seeking clarification on diagnostic studies and medication compliance. These moments are poignant reminders of the trust and confidence they place in me, highlighting the importance of patient education and empowerment in achieving positive health outcomes. Navigating these conversations with empathy and expertise reaffirms the transformative impact nurses can have in empowering individuals to take charge of their health journey.

Moreover, the opportunity to provide direct and indirect care to individuals I know personally adds a deeply fulfilling dimension to my practice. Each interaction becomes a testament to the interconnectedness of our lives and the profound impact we can have on one another. Whether offering a comforting word to a friend undergoing treatment or providing compassionate care to a family member in need, these moments highlight the deeply human aspect of nursing—the ability to connect personally and provide solace in times of vulnerability.

Beyond direct patient care, my role as a clinical nurse instructor has been equally rewarding. Guiding aspiring nurses through their educational journey and witnessing their growth and development firsthand fills me with immense pride and fulfillment. Watching students graduate and embark on their professional paths reaffirms my role in shaping the next generation of healthcare professionals.

As I mentor and support students, I am privileged to witness their transformation from eager learners to confident and compassionate nurses, equipped with the knowledge and skills to make a tangible difference in their patients' lives. Some of these students have

The Person I Became

stayed in touch, seeking professional development advice as they navigate their careers. Whether contemplating further education as a nurse practitioner, pursuing leadership roles, or specializing as a Certified Registered Nurse Anesthetist (CRNA), I am honored to offer guidance and support as they chart their course in the nursing profession.

The journey of nursing education is marked by both challenges and triumphs, setbacks and successes. As a clinical nurse instructor, I strive to create a nurturing and supportive learning environment where students feel empowered to explore their potential and overcome obstacles. Through mentorship, hands-on experience, and personalized guidance, I aim to instill in them the values of compassion, integrity, and lifelong learning—the pillars of nursing excellence.

In essence, my role as a nurse extends far beyond the confines of clinical practice; it encompasses a commitment to education, advocacy, and empowerment. Whether supporting patients on their healthcare journey or guiding aspiring nurses toward success, each day presents new opportunities to make a meaningful difference in the lives of others—a privilege I cherish deeply.

The Person I Became

Yet, the journey of self-discovery involves more than professional achievements; it also encompasses navigating the complexities of life, relationships, and personal identity. For me, this meant balancing the demands of work, education, and family responsibilities while staying true to my values and priorities. It involved confronting financial struggles and overcoming obstacles with resilience and perseverance.

One of the most challenging aspects of this journey was managing a full-time job while pursuing higher education in nursing. There were days when the demands felt overwhelming, leading to sleepless nights and countless hours spent on assignments and exam preparation. Despite the exhaustion, I was fueled by a desire to secure a better future for my family and to achieve my aspirations in the field of nursing.

Juggling the responsibilities of work, education, and family life often felt like trying to balance elephants on a tightrope. Each aspect of my life demanded attention and dedication, leaving me stretched thin and overwhelmed. The weight of each obligation felt like an elephant on my shoulders, threatening to topple me at any moment. It was a constant battle to keep all the plates spinning—meeting deadlines at work, excelling in my studies, and being present for my family. The stress was palpable, and I knew I needed to regain control before I was consumed by the chaos.

During this turbulent time, one of my mentors recommended a book that would profoundly impact my approach to managing these competing priorities: *Juggling Elephants*. This insightful read offered practical strategies and actionable tips for navigating the complexities of modern life while maintaining a sense of balance and sanity. What drew me to *Juggling Elephants* was not just its clever metaphor but its practical wisdom and actionable advice for managing competing priorities. The book provided a roadmap for establishing clear priorities, setting realistic expectations, and reclaiming balance amidst the chaos. It encouraged readers to assess their commitments, identify key areas of focus, and allocate time and resources accordingly—a paradigm shift that proved invaluable in my own journey.

As I delved deeper into the pages of *Juggling Elephants*, I began to view my situation with newfound clarity. I realized I couldn't continue managing all the responsibilities on my own without risking my well-being. I needed to prioritize self-care, set boundaries, and seek support from others to lighten the load. Guided by the book, I developed strategies for delegating tasks, saying no to non-essential commitments, and carving out dedicated time for rest and rejuvenation. Through its insights, I learned to identify my most important priorities—my mental health, delegating tasks when necessary, and setting boundaries to protect my time and energy.

Understanding the importance of work-life balance became a cornerstone of my approach to managing daily demands. I learned to honor my own needs and priorities, recognizing that self-care is not selfish but essential for maintaining overall well-being. By implementing the principles outlined in *Juggling Elephants*, I regained control over my schedule and found renewed energy and focus to tackle each day with purpose and clarity.

Moreover, *Juggling Elephants* taught me the value of replenishing my own cup amidst constant giving to others. I discovered the power of small acts of self-compassion, whether it was taking a leisurely walk in nature, watching Chelsea (my favorite soccer team) as a hobby, or simply pausing to breathe deeply and recalibrate my mindset. These moments of respite became essential pillars of my routine, serving as anchors of stability and grounding amidst life's whirlwind.

In essence, *Juggling Elephants* transformed my approach to managing the myriad responsibilities of work, education, and family life. It taught me to embrace the art of juggling with grace and intention, finding balance not through sheer force but through thoughtful prioritization and self-awareness. Armed with these newfound insights, I navigated the complexities of daily life with greater ease and confidence, staying true to myself while preserving my sanity amidst the chaos.

Central to this journey was my commitment to ensuring the happiness and comfort of my family, despite the challenges we faced. Balancing the needs of my spouse and children alongside my professional and academic pursuits required careful planning, open communication, and a willingness to adapt to changing circumstances.

My spouse initially felt neglected due to my focus on work and education, particularly during the days when I was away for extended periods. At first, I struggled with effective prioritization, but I soon realized that open communication was essential. By sharing my goals and explaining the reasons behind my commitments, I helped her understand my perspective and garnered her support.

Though my children were too young to express their feelings verbally, I observed subtle signs of distress in their behavior, especially in childcare settings. Acknowledging the impact my absence had on them, I made a deliberate effort to maximize the quality of our time together. I set aside phones and other distractions, focusing solely on being present with my family. We found joy in simple activities, like cooking together in the kitchen, where we bonded over shared experiences and created lasting memories. I took on tasks such as bathing and feeding the kids, even attempting to style their hair despite my lack of expertise. While my results might not have been perfect, the joy and appreciation in their faces made every effort worthwhile.

Through these intentional actions and heartfelt gestures, I gradually bridged the gap between my professional aspirations and my responsibilities as a spouse and parent. By prioritizing quality time and genuine connections with my family, I not only strengthened our bond but also found greater fulfillment and purpose in life.

In navigating the complexities of life, I have learned valuable lessons about resilience, adaptability, and the importance of prioritizing self-care. Each obstacle I encountered became an opportunity for growth, strengthening my resolve and deepening my understanding of my own capabilities. While the journey was fraught with challenges, it was also rich with moments of profound

The Person I Became

joy and fulfillment, as I witnessed the tangible impact of my efforts on both my family and my professional pursuits.

Through perseverance and determination, I emerged from this period of my life with a renewed sense of purpose and a deeper appreciation for the interconnectedness of work, education, and personal fulfillment. The journey of self-discovery continues to unfold, but with each step, I am reminded of the resilience of the human spirit and the transformative power of embracing life's complexities with courage and grace.

Amid these challenges, I discovered the transformative power of authenticity—the courage to embrace my true self, flaws and all, and to live life on my own terms. It was a journey of self-acceptance and self-love, learning to trust my instincts and follow my heart, even when the path ahead seemed uncertain. Reflecting on the defining moments of my journey, I am filled with gratitude for the lessons learned, the obstacles overcome, and the growth experienced along the way. Each setback was an opportunity for resilience, and each triumph was a testament to the power of perseverance and belief in oneself.

In the end, the journey of self-discovery is not merely about reaching a destination but about embracing the entire process—the ups and downs, the joys and sorrows, and finding meaning in every step along the way. It is about becoming the person we were always meant to be and inspiring others to embark on their own journey of self-discovery and empowerment.

As we continue on this journey together, I invite you to reflect on your own path—your challenges and triumphs—and to approach the journey of self-discovery with an open heart and a willingness to grow. For it is through embracing our true selves that we truly become who we are meant to be.

Chapter 2:
Balancing Act

Balancing work, education, and family life is a delicate dance—a complex choreography of responsibilities and commitments that often feels like navigating a maze without a clear path forward. This journey demands resilience, determination, and a deep understanding of one's priorities, coupled with the ability to adapt to life's ever-changing rhythm.

In the whirlwind of daily life, it's easy to get swept up by the relentless tide of tasks and obligations, leaving little time for self-care or personal fulfillment. Yet, it is precisely during these tumultuous times that self-care becomes crucial. As work and educational demands threaten to overwhelm, it's essential to carve out moments of respite and rejuvenation. Replenishing our own wellspring of energy and vitality allows us to give our best to those we love and to the tasks at hand.

Setting boundaries is another crucial aspect of navigating this delicate dance. It involves recognizing our limitations and honoring our own needs and priorities, even amidst external pressures or expectations. Whether it's saying no to additional commitments that encroach on our precious family time or setting aside dedicated moments for rest and relaxation amidst the chaos of daily life, boundaries act as guardrails that keep us grounded and centered.

Prioritizing one's well-being is perhaps the most important lesson from this journey. It means understanding that our happiness and fulfillment are intrinsically tied to our ability to care for ourselves—to nourish our bodies, minds, and spirits so that we can be fully present and engaged in every aspect of our lives. Whether it's taking a leisurely walk in nature, practicing mindfulness and meditation, or simply indulging in activities that bring us joy, prioritizing self-care is not a luxury but a necessity for maintaining balance and harmony amidst life's demands.

Ultimately, the journey of balancing work, education, and family life is a testament to the resilience of the human spirit and our capacity for growth and transformation, even in the most challenging circumstances. This journey teaches us to embrace the ebb and flow of life's rhythms, to navigate twists and turns with grace and fortitude, and to emerge stronger, wiser, and more resilient. Throughout it all, we are reminded of the importance of nurturing our own well-being, setting boundaries, and prioritizing self-care, so we can continue to dance through life with joy, purpose, and fulfillment.

For me, the balancing act began early in my career as I juggled the responsibilities of being a nurse while pursuing further education. It was a time of long hours, late nights, and seemingly endless to-do lists. Yet, amid the chaos, there was a profound sense of purpose—a drive to excel, to push beyond my limits, and to make a meaningful impact in the lives of others.

In my journey as a nurse, I have traversed a path marked by both triumphs and tribulations, each step shaping me into the healthcare professional I am today. My story is a tribute to the countless nurses who tirelessly serve on the frontlines of healthcare. Reflecting on the early days of my career, I remember the boundless energy and enthusiasm I brought to the nursing profession. Fresh out of nursing school, I was eager to make a difference in the lives of my patients, equipped with the knowledge and skills I had gained during my education. Little did I know that the challenges I would face would test me in ways I had never imagined.

Balancing the demands of work, education, and family life proved to be a formidable challenge—one that required a delicate blend of time management, prioritization, and self-care. As a nurse, I was accustomed to long hours, late nights, and the relentless pace of patient care. The weight of responsibility was palpable, yet amidst the chaos, a sense of purpose drove me forward.

As mentioned in the preceding chapter, one of the greatest challenges I faced early in my career was navigating the complexities of further education while working full-time as a nurse. Pursuing advanced degrees was a decision driven by a desire for personal and professional growth, but it came with its own set of hurdles. Balancing clinical responsibilities with coursework, assignments, and exams demanded meticulous planning and dedication. I found myself juggling multiple roles—nurse, student, parent, spouse—in a delicate dance that tested the limits of my endurance.

Yet, amidst the chaos, there were moments of clarity—instances when the pieces of the puzzle fell into place, and I saw the bigger picture. I realized that nursing is not just a job; it's a calling—a sacred duty to care for those in need and advocate for those who cannot advocate for themselves. The challenges I faced only strengthened my resolve, deepening my commitment to nursing.

The motivation to pursue further education in nursing was multifaceted, driven by a desire to expand my knowledge and skills, advance my career, and make a meaningful impact on my patients' lives. Pursuing advanced degrees offered opportunities for specialization, leadership, and research—opening doors to new possibilities and challenging the status quo. I recognized that the healthcare landscape was evolving rapidly, and as a nurse, it was my responsibility to stay ahead of the curve and adapt to changing trends and technologies.

As I delved deeper into my studies, I encountered a myriad of challenges—academic rigor, time constraints, and the constant juggling of work and school commitments. There were moments of doubt and uncertainty—times when I questioned whether I had taken on more than I could handle. Yet, each obstacle presented an opportunity for growth and self-discovery. I learned to embrace the journey, meeting both the highs and lows with equal parts humility and resilience.

One of the most valuable lessons I learned during this time was the importance of self-care and resilience. Nursing, by its very nature, is a demanding profession—one that requires physical, emotional, and mental fortitude. I quickly realized that I couldn't pour from an empty cup; I needed to prioritize my own well-being to provide the best possible care for my patients. I developed strategies for managing stress, staying organized, and maintaining a healthy work-life balance. Whether it was carving out time for exercise, meditation, or spending quality moments with loved ones, I made self-care a non-negotiable priority.

Building a support system was also crucial for navigating the challenges of further education and professional growth. My sister, Yanez, would be the go-to person to discuss personal matters. Colleagues, mentors, and supportive managers played instrumental roles in my journey, offering guidance, encouragement, and practical assistance when needed. One individual who stands out is Matilda Adams, my manager and mentor. Her support and mentorship were instrumental in helping me navigate the complexities of balancing work and school commitments. Her wisdom, guidance, and encouragement were invaluable as I charted my course in the nursing profession, and for that, I am eternally grateful.

The demands of the profession have often felt overwhelming, from long hours to emotional exhaustion. Yet, through it all, I have remained steadfast in my commitment to serving others and making a difference in the world. The difference could be something as simple as making someone smile.

In her book *Resilience,* Sandra Adom beautifully captures the essence of resilience—the ability to withstand adversity and emerge stronger on the other side. Reflecting on my own journey, I am reminded of Adom's words: "Resilience is not about avoiding hardship or pain, but rather about facing it head-on and finding the strength to overcome it." Indeed, my life's journey has been a testament to the resilience of the human spirit. It has been marked by highs and lows, triumphs and tribulations, but through it all, one thing has remained constant: my devotion to ensuring everyone around me does well.

Florence Nightingale once said, "Nursing is an art: and if it is to be made an art, it requires an exclusive devotion and preparation as rigorous as any painter's or sculptor's work." These words resonate deeply with me, serving as a constant reminder of the dedication and devotion required to excel in my chosen profession.

As I continue on this path, I am grateful for the privilege and honor of caring for those in need. Each day brings new challenges and opportunities for growth, but with dedication and determination, I am confident that I can make a meaningful impact on the lives of others. I am happy when I know everyone around me is doing well.

Navigating the complexities of work, education, and family life, I quickly realized the importance of prioritizing self-care. It's easy to become caught up in the hustle and bustle of everyday life and to put others' needs before our own. However, I learned that true strength lies in prioritizing self-care, the essential for maintaining balance and well-being.

The journey of prioritizing self-care began with a simple yet profound shift in perspective. I came to understand that caring for myself was not a selfish indulgence but a fundamental necessity for sustaining my ability to care for others. This realization was born out of necessity—a recognition that to continue serving my patients, supporting my family, and pursuing my educational goals, I needed to invest in my own physical, emotional, and mental health.

Exercise emerged as a cornerstone of my self-care routine, providing not only physical benefits but also serving as a powerful antidote to stress and tension. Whether it was a brisk walk in nature, a rejuvenating stretching session, or a heart-pounding workout at the gym while the kids participated in karate, I found solace and strength in the rhythm of movement. Each step, each stretch, became a form of self-expression—a tangible reminder of my commitment to honoring my body and soul.

Yet, self-care extended far beyond physical activity. It encompassed the art of relaxation, the practice of mindfulness, and the simple act of being present in the moment. I learned to carve out pockets of time amidst the chaos of daily life—moments of stillness and serenity where I could recharge and rejuvenate my spirit. Whether it was watching a movie, listening to music, playing FIFA on my PlayStation, cuddling up in my sauna bag, or simply relaxing in the backyard and enjoying the beauty of nature, I discovered the restorative power of intentional rest and relaxation.

Moreover, I realized that self-care was not just about setting aside time for myself, but also about cultivating a mindset of self-compassion and self-kindness. It was about embracing imperfection, celebrating progress, and honoring my own journey with grace and gratitude. I learned to silence the inner critic, to banish feelings of guilt or inadequacy, and to embrace the inherent worthiness of my own being.

In prioritizing self-care, I discovered a sense of empowerment—an understanding that my well-being was not contingent upon external circumstances or validation from others but was rather an intrinsic aspect of my own humanity. As I reflect on this journey, I am reminded of Audre Lorde's words: "Caring for myself is not self-indulgence, it is self-preservation, and that is an act of political warfare." In a world that often demands relentless productivity and self-sacrifice, prioritizing self-care is a radical act of resistance—

an affirmation of our inherent worth and a declaration of our right to thrive.

Prioritizing self-care is not just a luxury but a necessity—a fundamental aspect of sustaining balance, well-being, and resilience in the face of life's challenges. It reflects our commitment to honoring ourselves, nurturing our spirits, and embracing the fullness of our humanity. By doing so, we not only enrich our own lives but also create a ripple effect of healing and transformation that extends far beyond ourselves.

Self-care is a cornerstone of personal well-being, but it's only part of the equation. In addition to nurturing ourselves, it is imperative to establish boundaries and cultivate the ability to say no when necessary. As someone driven by a deep desire to help others, mastering the art of saying no was a formidable challenge—one that required a fundamental shift in perspective and a reevaluation of my own worth.

For much of my life, saying no felt synonymous with failure—an admission of weakness or inadequacy. Driven by a relentless desire to please others and a fear of disappointing those around me, I often overcommitted and stretched myself thin in an attempt to meet everyone's needs. In doing so, I inadvertently sacrificed my own well-being, neglecting my own needs and priorities.

Over time, however, I came to realize that saying no was not a sign of weakness but rather a sign of strength—a recognition of my own limits and a commitment to honoring my boundaries. It was a realization born out of assurance: to truly serve others and show up as my best self, I needed to prioritize my own needs and well-being. Learning to say no required a conscious effort to shift my mindset and redefine my relationship with boundaries. It meant acknowledging that my time, energy, and resources were finite and valuable—and that it was okay to allocate them in a way that aligned with my own priorities and values. It meant relinquishing the need for external validation and approval and instead embracing the inherent worthiness of my own needs and desires.

Yet, saying no was not always easy. It required courage, conviction, and a willingness to confront discomfort and uncertainty. There were moments of hesitation, doubt, and fear—but with each refusal came a newfound sense of empowerment and liberation. I began to recognize that by saying no to the things that did not serve me, I was saying yes to myself—to my well-being, my priorities, and my path.

Moreover, I discovered that setting boundaries and saying no not only preserved my well-being but also fostered healthier, more authentic relationships with those around me. By communicating my needs and limitations openly and honestly, I invited others to do the same, creating a space of mutual respect and understanding. I learned that true connection and collaboration thrive in an environment where each individual's needs and boundaries are honored and valued.

Navigating life's complexities and maintaining balance is a continuous journey fraught with challenges, especially when confronted with financial struggles or unexpected obstacles. There were moments when the demands of work, education, and family life seemed insurmountable, threatening to engulf me in a tidal wave of stress and uncertainty. Yet, amidst the chaos, I clung to a steadfast commitment to finding equilibrium, remaining true to myself, and confronting the journey with unwavering courage and resilience.

Financial literacy emerged as a beacon of hope amid the storm, offering invaluable insights into managing finances and navigating economic uncertainty. Delving into books like Dave Ramsey's *Total Money Makeover* and Robert Kiyosaki's *Rich Dad Poor Dad* (discussed further in subsequent chapters) proved transformative, shedding light on the nuances of financial management and dispelling misconceptions that had long plagued my understanding of money.

Through the wisdom imparted by these literary guides, I developed a newfound appreciation for the importance of financial literacy in achieving stability and security. Concepts such as distinguishing between good debt and bad debt, understanding the value of assets versus liabilities, and mastering the art of budgeting and saving became foundational pillars of my financial journey.

Moreover, I learned to approach financial challenges with a sense of empowerment and intervention, rather than succumbing to feelings of helplessness or overwhelm. Armed with knowledge and understanding, I faced debt with a renewed sense of purpose, devising strategic plans to eliminate financial burdens and forge a path toward financial freedom.

Yet, the journey toward financial literacy was not without its hurdles. It required discipline, dedication, and a willingness to confront uncomfortable truths about my financial habits and behaviors. There were moments of frustration and setbacks, but with each obstacle came an opportunity for growth and learning, ultimately steering me toward a brighter financial future.

In the midst of financial turmoil, I discovered the transformative power of financial literacy—a tool that not only empowered me to take control of my financial destiny but also instilled a sense of confidence and resilience in the face of adversity—a journey that continues to unfold with each passing day.

As I reflect on this journey, I am reminded of Warren Buffett's wisdom: "The best investment you can make is in yourself." Indeed, investing in financial literacy has yielded dividends far beyond monetary value, equipping me with the knowledge and skills needed to navigate life's financial terrain with confidence and clarity. However, it's the investment in my own health is what mattered. I've come to realize that financial literacy is not just about managing money; it's about empowering oneself to build a life of stability, security, and abundance. It's about reclaiming control over one's financial destiny and forging a path toward a brighter, more prosperous future. Embracing the financial literacy journey unlocks a world of possibility, empowerment, and financial well-being.

As I reflect on the balancing act that has defined my journey, I am filled with gratitude for the lessons learned, the obstacles overcome, and the growth experienced along the way. This journey

The Person I Became

has taught me the importance of self-care, setting boundaries, and prioritizing my own well-being, and it continues to shape who I am today. So, as we continue on this journey together, I invite you to reflect on your own balancing act, your own challenges and triumphs, and to embrace the journey with courage, resilience, and a deep sense of self-awareness. It is through embracing the complexities of life that we truly find balance, and through finding balance that we discover peace, joy, and contentment.

The Person I Became

Chapter 3: Lessons Learned

Life is a journey of continuous learning—a series of lessons that shape our perspectives, attitudes, and actions. As I reflect on my own journey, I am humbled by the wisdom and insight gained from the challenges faced, the triumphs celebrated, and the moments of growth experienced along the way.

One of the most profound lessons I've learned is the importance of resilience in the face of adversity. Life is unpredictable, and challenges are inevitable. Whether encountering setbacks in my career, navigating personal hardships, or confronting unexpected obstacles, I've realized that resilience is the key to weathering life's storms. It is the ability to bounce back, to find strength in adversity, and to emerge much stronger than before.

The journey of life is filled with uncertainties and challenges, each bringing its own set of obstacles and trials. Yet, amidst the unpredictability, one of the most reflective lessons I've learned is the indispensable value of resilience. This quality goes beyond mere survival, instilling us with the strength and tenacity to weather life's storms and emerge stronger on the other side.

The Person I Became

I've come to realize that resilience is not just about enduring hardships—it's about thriving despite them. It's the dense resolve to confront adversity head-on, draw on inner strength in the face of overwhelming odds, and transform moments of despair into opportunities for growth and renewal.

Throughout my journey, I have faced numerous setbacks and challenges—moments of doubt, fear, and uncertainty that threatened to derail my progress and shatter my resolve. Whether navigating the complexities of my career, grappling with personal hardships, or confronting unexpected obstacles, resilience has been my steadfast companion, guiding me through the darkest times and propelling me toward the light.

In moments of adversity, I've learned to draw upon reservoirs of inner strength, tapping into a wellspring of courage and determination I never knew existed. It's during these trials that I've discovered the true depth of my own strength—the capacity to endure, persevere, and rise above challenges that once seemed insurmountable. This trait demands a willingness to confront discomfort and uncertainty, to view failure as an opportunity for growth, and to face life's challenges with optimism and resolve.

The Person I Became

In these hard times, I've found solace and strength in the support of loved ones, colleagues, and mentors who have lifted me and reminded me of my inherent strength. Their encouragement, guidance, and belief in my abilities have been instrumental in helping me navigate life's trials and emerge stronger always.

As I reflect on my journey, I'm reminded of the words of resilience researcher Brené Brown, who writes, "The only constant in life is change. Resilience is accepting that life is full of setbacks and choosing to rise above them."

My journey of endurance has been one of transformation and growth—It is a journey defined by courage and unwavering determination, one that continues to unfold with each passing day, empowering us to navigate life's trials and emerge stronger, wiser, and more resilient than before.

I have come to deeply appreciate the value of perseverance—the steadfast commitment to pursuing our goals and dreams, even when faced with obstacles and setbacks. In moments of doubt and uncertainty, perseverance keeps us moving forward, fueling our determination to overcome challenges and achieve success. It is our belief in ourselves and in our ability to conquer adversity that propels us along our journey.

The Person I Became

Perseverance, the unwavering dedication to our dreams and aspirations despite the inevitable challenges, has shaped my path. During times of doubt and uncertainty, perseverance has been my guiding light, illuminating the way forward and instilling within me the courage and determination to keep pressing on.

Perseverance is not a passive trait; it is an active choice—a conscious decision to persist despite adversity, to refuse to be deterred by obstacles or setbacks. It is the relentless commitment to keep moving forward, step by step, even when the road ahead seems long and arduous. This trait is deeply rooted in self-belief—a conviction that we can overcome any obstacle that stands in our way.

In my own journey, perseverance has been both a beacon of hope and a source of strength. It has carried me through moments of doubt and despair, empowering me to overcome obstacles that once seemed impossible. It has fueled my determination to pursue my passions and aspirations, even in the face of daunting challenges. But perseverance is not without its challenges. Yet, it is precisely in these moments that the true power of perseverance becomes evident. It is then that we must dig deep, draw upon our inner reserves of strength and resilience, and press on with untiring determination.

The Person I Became

As I reflect on my journey, I am reminded of Winston Churchill's words: "Success is not final, failure is not fatal: It is the courage to continue that counts." Indeed, it is the courage to persevere in the face of adversity, to keep striving for our goals and dreams, that ultimately defines our success.

Another crucial lesson I've learned is the power of adaptability—the ability to embrace change, pivot in the face of uncertainty, and thrive in ever-evolving circumstances. In a world that is continuously shifting, adaptability is essential for navigating life's challenges and seizing new opportunities. Whether adjusting to changes in the workplace, relationships, or personal circumstances, the capacity to welcome change with an open mind and a willingness to learn is vital for growth and success.

Adaptability, often defined as the ability to adjust and thrive in response to changing circumstances, has become a cornerstone of my journey. It is a lesson learned through experience, reshaping my perspective and transforming the way I navigate life's ever-shifting landscape. It's about proactively embracing opportunities for growth and transformation. It involves cultivating a mindset of flexibility and resilience that allows us to pivot in the face of uncertainty and emerge stronger on the other side. Change is not something to be feared or resisted but embraced as an inevitable human experience. In a world marked by constant change and uncertainty, adaptability is not merely a desirable trait—it is an indispensable skill. It empowers us to approach life's challenges head on. As Charles Darwin wisely said, "It is not the strongest of the species that survives, nor the most intelligent, but the most adaptable to change." I am grateful for the lessons learned and the growth opportunities that come with embracing change with an open heart and mind.

An additional important lesson I've learned is the transformative power of positivity—the ability to maintain a positive mindset even in the darkest times and find the silver lining in every situation. Positivity is about recognizing the inherent goodness in the world, appreciating the beauty in everyday moments, and uncovering the potential for growth and transformation in every challenge.

By cultivating a positive mindset, I've approached life's challenges with optimism and flexibility, drawing strength and inspiration from adversity. The power of positivity has been a beacon of light in my journey—a guiding force that has illuminated the darkest times and infused even the most challenging moments with hope and strength.

The Person I Became

Throughout my journey, I have faced countless moments of darkness and despair—times when it felt like the weight of the world was pressing down on my shoulders, threatening to crush my spirit and extinguish my hope. Yet, in those moments, it was the power of positivity that sustained me, lifting me up and guiding me through the storm.

Positivity is not a passive state of mind—it's a conscious choice and a daily practice that demands dedication and effort. It involves reframing negative thoughts, challenging pessimistic attitudes, and embracing a mindset of possibility and abundance. It also means surrounding oneself with positivity and seeking inspiration and encouragement in the world around us.

In the words of Winston Churchill, "The pessimist sees difficulty in every opportunity. The optimist sees opportunity in every difficulty." Indeed, positivity is not just a state of mind—it's a way of life. As I continue on my journey, I am grateful for the transformative power of positivity. It has empowered me to overcome adversity, find strength in challenges, and embrace life with joy and resilience.

Another crucial aspect of my journey has been the realization that success is not a destination but a journey—a process of self-discovery, personal growth, and continuous learning. I've learned that success is not measured by accolades or material possessions but by the impact we make in the world around us, the lives we touch, and the legacy we leave behind. It's about using our talents and passions to make a meaningful difference, leaving the world better than we found it.

By setting ambitious goals and remaining focused on my vision for the future, I've achieved notable success at a young age. My journey has been marked by milestones such as obtaining my nursing degree, advancing my education to earn a doctorate, and starting my own business. Yet, beyond these accomplishments lies a deeper sense of fulfillment—one that comes from knowing I am making a positive impact in the world and leaving a legacy.

One of my most significant contributions to the nursing field has been through my tutoring business, EZ2PASSNCLEX LLC. This venture has allowed me to help countless students succeed on the NCLEX, the licensure examination for nurses. By offering affordable and sometimes free tutoring sessions, I've been able to eliminate financial barriers and ensure that students have access to the support they need to achieve their goals.

In these tutoring sessions, I focus not only on imparting test-taking strategies and techniques but also on helping students break down complex questions and grasp key nursing concepts. Beyond academic support, I aim to build confidence and resilience in my students, empowering them to tackle the NCLEX challenges with courage and determination.

The impact of my tutoring business has been profound. Students frequently reach out to express their gratitude for the support and guidance I've provided. This feedback is a testament to the power of mentorship and the transformative impact one person can have on the lives of others.

My journey of success has been defined not just by the accomplishments I've achieved but by the impact I've made and the lives I've touched along the way. It's a journey driven by ambition, passion, and a relentless commitment to making a difference in the world. As I continue on this path, I am grateful for the opportunity to contribute to the nursing field and to leave a legacy of empowerment and inspiration for future generations.

Perhaps the most profound lesson of all is the importance of embracing the journey itself—its ups and downs, twists and turns, and moments of joy and sorrow. Life is not always easy, and there are no guarantees of success or happiness. Yet, it is through the journey that we find meaning, purpose, and fulfillment. It is in facing challenges, learning lessons, and forging connections that we truly discover the depth of our purpose and the richness of our experiences.

Embracing the journey itself has been a lesson that has transformed my perspective on life, instilling every moment with deeper meaning and significance. This lesson has emerged from the myriad experiences of joy and sorrow, triumph and tribulation, which have painted the canvas of my existence.

In a world where success is often measured by external achievements and material possessions, it's easy to overlook the beauty and richness of the journey itself. Yet, I've come to understand that true fulfillment lies not in reaching a destination, but in savoring the journey along the way. It's about finding joy in the small moments, embracing challenges as opportunities for growth, and cherishing the connections we forge with others.

Embracing the journey goes beyond accepting the highs and lows—it involves actively engaging with life and seizing every opportunity for growth and transformation. It's about stepping out of our comfort zones, taking risks, and embracing the unknown with courage and curiosity. It's about living fully, with passion, purpose, and a sense of adventure.

As I reflect on my journey, I am reminded of the poet Mary Oliver's words: "Tell me, what is it you plan to do with your one wild and precious life?" Indeed, life is a precious gift—a journey to be embraced with open arms and hearts. In embracing this journey, with all its beauty and complexity, we find true meaning, purpose, and fulfillment.

In addition to resilience, perseverance, adaptability, and positivity, I've learned the importance of personal growth and development. Personal growth extends beyond acquiring new skills or knowledge; it's about becoming the best version of ourselves, acknowledging our strengths and weaknesses, and continually striving for self-improvement. Whether through formal education, self-reflection, or new experiences, personal growth is vital for living a fulfilling and meaningful life. It's a lesson learned through introspection, exploration, and a dedication to lifelong learning.

One pivotal aspect of personal growth is cultivating self-awareness—a profound understanding of our own thoughts, feelings, and behaviors. By developing self-awareness, we gain insight into our strengths and weaknesses and understand how our actions affect both ourselves and others. This heightened awareness enables us to make more intentional choices and navigate life's challenges with greater clarity and purpose.

In "Emotional Intelligence," Daniel Goleman delves into the concept of emotional intelligence as a crucial element of personal growth. Goleman defines emotional intelligence as the capacity to recognize, understand, and manage our emotions and those of others. By refining our emotional intelligence skills, we can handle interpersonal relationships more effectively, communicate more authentically, and resolve conflicts more easily.

Formal education has been a cornerstone of my personal growth journey. Pursuing higher education has not only broadened my knowledge and skills but also challenged me to think critically, communicate effectively, and collaborate with others. It has equipped me with the tools and resources to face life's challenges with confidence and resilience.

But personal growth extends far beyond the classroom—it's a lifelong pursuit that goes beyond formal education. It involves seeking new experiences, pushing ourselves out of our comfort zones, and embracing the unknown with courage and curiosity. Personal growth and development are vital for living a fulfilling and meaningful life. By embracing the journey of self-discovery and transformation, we unlock our full potential, cultivate healthy relationships, and find purpose and fulfillment. As I continue my path, I am dedicated to treating personal growth as a lifelong pursuit, constantly striving to become the best version of myself and make a positive impact in the world.

Each experience, whether positive or negative, has contributed to who I am today, and for that, I am truly thankful. I remember Maya Angelou's words: "I can be changed by what happens to me. But I refuse to be reduced by it." It is through embracing the journey that we find the strength to overcome life's challenges and emerge much stronger than before.

As we journey together, take a moment to reflect on the lessons learned in your own life. Embrace resilience, pursue personal growth, and cultivate emotional intelligence. May these lessons guide you toward fulfillment, purpose, and a lasting impact on your path of continuous learning.

Chapter 4: Guided by Mentorship

Mentorship is a guiding light on the journey of personal and professional growth—a beacon of wisdom, support, and inspiration that illuminates the path forward. Throughout my journey, I have been fortunate to receive the guidance of mentors who have greatly shaped the person I am today.

My journey with mentorship began with a deep appreciation for the value of learning from those who had walked the path before me. From the earliest days of my nursing career, I understood the importance of seeking out mentors who could offer wisdom, share their experiences, and provide crucial support as I navigated the complexities of the healthcare profession. These mentors were not merely guides; they were trusted advisors, confidants, and champions who believed in my potential and encouraged me to reach for the stars.

As I reflect on the pivotal role mentorship has played in shaping my journey, I am reminded of the qualities I sought in my mentors: wisdom tempered with humility, empathy combined with resilience, and a genuine commitment to nurturing the next generation of healthcare professionals. These mentors not only possessed extensive knowledge and expertise in their fields but also embodied the values of compassion, integrity, and lifelong learning—hallmarks of exemplary healthcare providers.

Through their guidance and support, I was able to navigate the complexities of patient care, develop critical clinical skills, and deepen my understanding of the ethical and moral responsibilities inherent in nursing. Moreover, they instilled in me a sense of confidence and self-assurance, empowering me to advocate for my patients' well-being and to tackle the numerous challenges and uncertainties that come with a healthcare career.

But perhaps most importantly, my mentors served as beacons of inspiration, illuminating the path ahead and igniting a passion for lifelong learning and professional growth within me. Their unwavering belief in my potential fueled my determination to excel, motivating me to pursue further education, seek out leadership opportunities, and embrace new challenges with courage and conviction.

My journey with mentorship was influenced by individuals like Tahitia Timmons, whose wisdom and guidance shaped my career in unexpected and transformative ways. As a new nurse, Tahitia challenged me to adopt a mindset of lifelong learning—a commitment to continuous growth and development that became the cornerstone of my professional journey.

Tahitia's words, urging me never to stop learning, resonated deeply, instilling within me a sense of curiosity and a hunger for knowledge that propelled my career forward. Through her mentorship, I learned that true excellence in nursing is not merely a destination but a journey—a journey defined by a relentless pursuit of knowledge, skill refinement, and personal growth.

Later in my career, Tahitia presented me with a new challenge: to venture into the realm of editing. It was a daunting prospect, requiring me to step outside my comfort zone and embrace a new set of skills and responsibilities. Yet, guided by Tahitia's unwavering belief in my abilities, I embraced the opportunity wholeheartedly.

Working for Lippincott Professional Development, where I wrote and reviewed competency courses, became a pivotal moment in my career—a testament to the transformative power of mentorship and the importance of embracing new challenges. Under Tahitia's guidance, I honed my editing skills, expanded my professional horizons, and gained invaluable insights into curriculum development and educational design for professional nurses. Through this experience, I learned that mentorship is not merely about imparting knowledge or providing guidance; it is about empowering individuals to unlock their full potential, embrace new opportunities, and chart a course toward professional fulfillment and success. Tahitia Timmons embodied this ethos, challenging me to push beyond my limits, explore uncharted territories, and uncover the untapped potential within me.

As I reflect on the deep impact of Tahitia's mentorship on my journey, I am reminded of the ripple effect of mentorship—the way a single act of guidance and encouragement can resonate through the lives of others, inspiring greatness and catalyzing positive change. It is a legacy I strive to honor daily as I pay forward the invaluable lessons and insights I have received, nurturing the next generation of healthcare professionals and empowering them to reach for the stars.

In Tahitia Timmons, I found a beacon of inspiration—a guiding light whose wisdom and guidance continue to illuminate my path. Her belief in my potential, support, and willingness to challenge me to grow and evolve has left an indelible mark on my journey. This mark is a constant reminder of the transformative power of mentorship and the boundless possibilities within each of us.

The Person I Became

As I advanced in my career, I had the privilege of paying forward the invaluable lessons and insights imparted by my mentors. Serving as a mentor to aspiring nurses and healthcare professionals, I strive to embody the same qualities of wisdom, empathy, and support that were given to me. Whether offering guidance on clinical practice, career advancement, or personal development, I am committed to nurturing the next generation of healthcare leaders and instilling in them the values of compassion, integrity, and excellence that are the cornerstones of our profession.

In a world characterized by constant change and evolving challenges, the role of mentorship in shaping the future of healthcare cannot be overstated. As we embark on this journey of mentorship—both as mentors and mentees—let us remain steadfast in our commitment to learning, growing, and uplifting one another.

One of the most impactful lessons I learned from my mentors was the transformative power of self-belief—a lesson that shaped the course of my career and infused every aspect of my journey with newfound confidence and determination. In moments of self-doubt or uncertainty, my mentors stood as unwavering pillars of support, offering encouragement and wisdom that resonated deeply within me.

The Person I Became

Their belief in my abilities was a beacon of inspiration, illuminating the path ahead and emboldening me to pursue my dreams with steadfast resolve. Matilda Adams, in particular, played a pivotal role in nurturing this belief, challenging me to embrace leadership roles that tested the limits of my capabilities.

Under Matilda's mentorship, I was entrusted with chairing a unit-based council (UBC)—a responsibility that proved both daunting and exhilarating. Within our UBC, we led initiatives to enhance patient care and safety, including the development of innovative fall prevention protocols and the implementation of acuity-based tools for equitable patient assignment.

Leading the UBC technology implementation team was a particularly defining moment in my journey. This role not only sharpened my leadership skills but also opened doors to new opportunities in the expanding field of nursing informatics. With Matilda's guidance and support, I pursued further education and earned my Master of Science in Nursing (MSN) in Informatics—a milestone that facilitated my transition into clinical transformation.

As I ventured into the realm of clinical transformation, I was presented with the opportunity to serve as a clinical transformational specialist—a role that allowed me to leverage my expertise in informatics to drive meaningful change within healthcare organizations. However, as I navigated the demands of this role, I found myself at a crossroads, grappling with the challenge of balancing professional aspirations with familial responsibilities.

During this pivotal moment, I leaned on the wisdom of my mentors, drawing strength from their guidance. Although the prospect of a clinical analyst position was highly appealing, I ultimately decided to prioritize my family's needs, recognizing that the demands of the role would be incompatible with my familial obligations.

In hindsight, this decision highlighted the invaluable lessons I had learned from my mentors—the importance of staying true to oneself, prioritizing what truly matters, and embracing the journey with courage and certainty. Their belief in my abilities empowered me to navigate my career's complexities with grace and resilience, guiding me toward a path aligned with my values and aspirations.

As I continue to chart my course in the ever-evolving landscape of healthcare, I am reminded of the profound impact of mentorship. In Matilda Adams and mentors like her, I found not only advisors but champions of my potential whose belief in me continues to inspire greatness and catalyze positive change.

As I advanced in my career, I found myself able to offer support and guidance to individuals just beginning their venture into nursing. Whether through formal mentorship programs or informal conversations over coffee, I embraced the opportunity to share my experiences, offer advice, and inspire the next generation of nurses.

Mentorship became a cornerstone of my professional philosophy—an opportunity to give back to a profession that had given me so much. I mentored aspiring nurses, encouraging them to take the initiative and pursue their nursing dreams with determination and passion. Through my guidance, they gained the confidence to navigate the complexities of nursing education and embark on a career path filled with endless possibilities.

Family members also sought my guidance and mentorship as they ventured into the world of nursing. I provided support, sharing insights from my journey and offering practical advice to help them navigate the challenges of nursing education and licensure. Together, we celebrated their triumphs and addressed their setbacks, forging bonds that extended beyond familial ties.

Additionally, I extended my mentorship across borders, assisting individuals transitioning into the nursing field from overseas. I guided them through the complexities of degree evaluation and appraisal, offering support as they prepared for the NCLEX examination. Through this experience, I witnessed firsthand the transformative power of mentorship in overcoming cultural barriers and empowering individuals to pursue their nursing passion on a global scale.

As a mentor, I am deeply committed to fostering a culture of continuous learning and professional development among my mentees. Embracing new opportunities, expanding horizons, and advancing degrees are essential steps toward realizing one's full potential in the nursing profession. Whether through formal continuing education programs, professional development initiatives, or leadership opportunities, I encourage my mentees to pursue avenues for growth and self-improvement actively.

I am particularly passionate about guiding and supporting my mentees in advancing their nursing education. With the increasing demand for highly skilled and knowledgeable nursing educators, I recognize the critical importance of nurturing the next generation of nurse educators. I urge some of my mentees to consider pursuing advanced degrees in nursing education, emphasizing the pivotal role they can play in shaping the future of nursing through teaching, mentorship, and research.

One aspect of mentoring that brings me particular joy is working with new nurse educators. Recognizing the unique challenges and opportunities they face in transitioning from clinical practice to academia, I developed a mentoring handbook to guide novice nurse educators through their journey to advanced levels of expertise. This handbook serves as a comprehensive resource, offering practical strategies, tips, and best practices for navigating the complexities of the educational landscape and fostering excellence in teaching and mentorship.

Through this handbook, I aim to empower new nurse educators with the knowledge, skills, and confidence they need to excel in their roles and make a meaningful impact on the next generation of nurses. My mentorship covers topics such as curriculum development, classroom management, assessment strategies, and faculty engagement to support novice educators at every stage of their professional development. Moreover, my approach to mentoring extends beyond traditional relationships. I strive to create a supportive and inclusive learning environment where mentees feel empowered to ask questions, seek guidance, and explore their interests and passions. Through open communication, active listening, and personalized support, I foster a collaborative partnership with my mentees, guiding them toward their goals with empathy, respect, and enthusiasm.

My commitment to mentorship is rooted in a deep belief in the transformative power of education and mentorship in shaping the future of nursing. By empowering individuals to pursue advanced degrees, develop their teaching skills, and become effective mentors themselves, I aim to create a ripple effect of positive change that extends well beyond our immediate interactions. Together, we can inspire greatness, foster innovation, and cultivate a community of lifelong learners dedicated to advancing the art and science of nursing.

Mentorship is a reciprocal journey—a symbiotic relationship where both mentor and mentee learn, grow, and evolve together. As I continue to pay forward the invaluable lessons and insights I have received, I am reminded of the profound impact mentorship has in shaping the future of nursing. Through our collective efforts, we have the power to inspire greatness, catalyze positive change, and leave a lasting legacy that transcends time and space.

In addition to professional mentorship, I've been fortunate to have personal mentors who have guided me on my path of personal growth and self-discovery. Reflecting on the role of mentorship in my journey, I am grateful for those who have been there for me. Their wisdom, support, and encouragement have consistently inspired me, helping me navigate life's complexities and achieve success both personally and professionally. As I move forward, I am committed to paying it forward by serving as a mentor to others, understanding that the greatest gift we can offer is guidance and support to those who need it most. So, as we continue on this journey together, I invite you to reflect on your own acts of mentorship.

Chapter 5: From Struggles to Success

Navigating life's journey is like traversing a winding road, full of peaks and valleys, unexpected detours, and unforeseen challenges. My own path to success has been no different, woven with a tapestry of experiences that include both triumphs and setbacks. Along this journey, I've faced daunting obstacles and embarked on a quest for self-discovery that has tested my very core. Yet, amid the turbulence and uncertainty, I've learned that it is not the circumstances we encounter, but how we respond to them, that ultimately defines our journey.

It is in our darkest moments, when doubt looms large and the path ahead appears shrouded in uncertainty, that we unearth our latent potential. It is through these challenges that we rise above, emerging stronger and wiser than before. Each setback I've encountered has been a catalyst for growth—a crucible in which I've forged the strength and tenacity needed to navigate life's ever-changing landscape. Through adversity, I've learned the importance of adaptability and the power of a positive mindset in overcoming obstacles and seizing opportunities for growth.

The Person I Became

Most importantly, I've come to understand that the absence of challenges does not define success, but by our ability to harness the lessons learned from adversity and transform them into opportunities for personal and professional development.

In the grand tapestry of life, our response to adversity shapes the narrative of our journey, imbues our experiences with meaning and purpose, and ultimately defines the legacy we leave behind. As we navigate the twists and turns of life, let us embrace the challenges that come our way, draw strength from the depths of our resilience, and move forward with unwavering determination. It is through overcoming obstacles that we truly grow and thrive.

One of the most daunting challenges I encountered was financial insecurity early in my journey. As a young adult, I was thrust into the complexities of balancing work, education, and family responsibilities while grappling with financial instability. It felt as though every step forward was met with an obstacle, and the looming specter of uncertainty overshadowed every glimmer of hope.

Navigating the tumultuous waters of financial insecurity tested my ability to make tough decisions in the face of adversity. One of my greatest struggles during this time was my difficulty in saying no when others sought my help. Driven by a desire to see others succeed, I often extended a helping hand at the expense of my own financial well-being. While my intentions were noble, this tendency to prioritize others needs over my own led to the mismanagement of my budget and worsened the burden of financial strain.

There were moments when it felt as though the weight of financial insecurity would crush me beneath its relentless pressure. Bills piled up, expenses mounted, and the prospect of achieving financial stability seemed like an elusive dream. Yet, amid the darkness of despair, I came to understand that I could not pour from an empty cup. This affirmed that, by taking care of myself, I can better serve those around me.

Slowly but surely, I began to reclaim control over my financial destiny. Through careful budgeting, strategic planning, and disciplined saving, I charted a course toward financial stability—one small step at a time. Along the way, I discovered that financial security is not merely a destination but a journey marked continuous adaptation to the tides of life.

Looking back on those early struggles, I am reminded of the profound resilience of the human spirit—the ability to endure,

The Person I Became

overcome, and emerge victorious in the face of adversity. While the scars of financial insecurity may still linger, they stand as a testament to the strength and fortitude within each of us. Though the journey was challenging, the lessons learned have transformed me into a stronger, more resilient, and compassionate individual—one who is better equipped to face whatever challenges lie ahead.

I consciously decided to defy despair and believe in the power of possibility. Instead of letting financial insecurity dictate my life's course, I embarked on a journey of self-discovery and empowerment, seeking opportunities for personal and professional growth that would lead me toward a brighter future.

One of the first steps I took was to engage in open and honest discussions with friends and loved ones about the challenges posed by the economy and inflation, which exacerbated our financial struggles. These conversations were a mix of emotions—some stories were lighthearted and funny, while others were gut-wrenching and deeply personal. Through these shared experiences, we discovered that many of us had a common tendency to overstretch ourselves to please those around us, often digging ourselves deeper into financial difficulties.

The Person I Became

Sharing our experiences and insights proved to be a pivotal moment in my journey toward financial stability. By opening up about our challenges, we offered each other support, encouragement, and practical advice for navigating the turbulent waters of financial instability. These discussions fostered a sense of camaraderie and solidarity as we realized we were not alone in our struggles.

We celebrated small victories, such as sticking to a budget for a month or finding a side hustle that brought in extra money. We also tackled bigger challenges, like managing mounting debts or facing unexpected expenses that threatened to derail our financial plans. These honest conversations helped us view our financial situations more clearly and understand that the path to financial freedom was not a solitary journey but a shared experience with those around us.

Through these exchanges, we implemented practical strategies to regain control over our finances. We encouraged each other to use budgeting tools, track our spending, and set realistic financial goals. We also shared tips on cutting costs, finding additional sources of income, and avoiding unnecessary spending. The collective wisdom and support from these discussions became a vital resource, empowering us to take actionable steps toward improving our financial situations.

Engaging in these discussions was not just about sharing advice but about creating a support and accountability network. Knowing that we had a community of friends and loved ones who understood our struggles and were committed to helping each other succeed made a significant difference in our journey toward financial stability. This support network became a source of strength and motivation, helping us stay focused in facing financial challenges.

In my quest for financial stability, I turned to resources like Dave Ramsey's *The Total Money Makeover:* A Proven Plan for Financial Fitness for guidance and inspiration. Ramsey's practical and actionable advice gave me invaluable insights into budgeting, saving, and managing debt, laying the groundwork for a more secure financial future.

The Total Money Makeover challenged me to rethink my approach to money management and adopt a new mindset focused on discipline, responsibility, and long-term financial success. Drawing on Ramsey's "Baby Steps" approach, I learned the importance of creating a budget, living below my means, and prioritizing debt repayment as crucial steps toward financial independence.

One of the most impactful aspects of Ramsey's methodology was his emphasis on living debt-free. By following his step-by-step plan for debt elimination, I was able to break free from the constraints of consumer debt and regain control over my financial future. Ramsey's mantra, "Live like no one else now, so you can live like no one else later," became a guiding principle in my journey toward financial freedom. Ramsey's focus on the importance of emergency savings and building a robust financial safety net resonated deeply with me. His guidance helped me establish an emergency fund to cover unexpected expenses and weather financial storms, providing me with peace of mind and security during times of uncertainty.

Another resource I used in my pursuit of financial freedom is Robert Kiyosaki's groundbreaking book *Rich Dad Poor Dad*. Drawing on Kiyosaki's insights and wisdom, I gained a deeper understanding of the fundamental principles of wealth-building and financial independence. *Rich Dad Poor Dad* challenged conventional wisdom and offered a fresh perspective on money, investing, and the path to financial success.

The Person I Became

One of the key lessons I gleaned from *Rich Dad Poor Dad* was the concept of shifting from a mindset of consumption to one of investment—a paradigm shift that has greatly impacted my approach to money management. By prioritizing assets that generate income and appreciate in value over time, I have been able to build a solid financial foundation and create opportunities for wealth accumulation and abundance.

Moreover, Kiyosaki's emphasis on financial education and entrepreneurship resonated deeply with me, inspiring me to take proactive steps toward enhancing my financial literacy and exploring avenues for income generation beyond traditional employment. Armed with the knowledge and insights gained from *Rich Dad Poor Dad,* I embarked on a journey of self-discovery and empowerment, determined to break free from the constraints of financial insecurity and chart a course toward financial freedom.

Incorporating Ramsey's principles into my financial strategy, alongside resources like Robert Kiyosaki's *Rich Dad Poor Dad*, provided me with a comprehensive framework for achieving my goals and aspirations.

Over time, I began to see the fruits of my labor as my financial situation gradually improved. Through discipline and determination, I was able to manage debt effectively, build a robust emergency fund, and confidently invest in my future. Each milestone achieved became a testament to the power of goal setting and the transformative potential of commitment.

Perhaps the greatest reward of all was the sense of empowerment that came from taking control of my financial destiny. No longer shackled by the burden of uncertainty, I found freedom in knowing that I had the power to shape my future and create the life I desired.

Another significant struggle I faced on my journey was balancing work, education, and family responsibilities. As a nurse, I navigated the demands of a challenging career while pursuing further education and raising a family. This juggling act required meticulous planning, effective time management, and a willingness to prioritize my goals and aspirations.

Amidst the chaos of daily life, I found moments of clarity, inspiration, and growth. I discovered the transformative power of adaptability and maintaining a positive outlook in the face of adversity. These qualities became the foundation upon which I built my journey, allowing me to navigate life's challenges with grace and strength.

The Person I Became

A positive mindset allowed me to inspire and uplift those around me. By modeling resilience, adaptability, and optimism, I encouraged others to embrace these qualities in their own lives. This ripple effect fostered a supportive and empowering environment where we could all pursue our goals with confidence and determination.

Amidst the chaos of daily life, I found moments of clarity, inspiration, and growth that transformed my journey. In the end, the journey from struggles to success is not just about reaching a destination—it's about embracing the process, the ups and downs, the challenges and triumphs, and finding meaning and purpose in every step of the way.

Success is what we see from looking within. It doesn't have to look like what others have. It is about being content with what we have, giving back to the community, and helping or guiding others to achieve their simplest goals. The most important thing is giving thanks and showing appreciation to family and friends for the support they provide. As I continue on my journey, I am grateful for the struggles I've faced, the lessons I've learned, and the growth I've experienced along the way. I am excited for the opportunities that lie ahead and I urge you to reflect on your journey from struggles to success.

Chapter 6:
The Power of Voice and Influence

In our life journey, our voice is the thread that weaves together our experiences, emotions, and aspirations. It is the instrument through which we express our deepest thoughts, heartfelt desires, and unwavering convictions. Our voice is our most powerful tool—capable of inspiring, empowering, and effecting positive change in the world around us. For me, discovering the power of my voice was a transformative moment—a realization that my words could uplift, inspire, and make a meaningful difference in the lives of others. It was a journey of self-discovery, finding the courage to speak my truth, and embracing the power of authenticity with conviction and grace.

One of the earliest lessons I learned about the power of voice was the importance of confidence—confidence in oneself, one's abilities, and one's voice. In a world that often seeks to silence or diminish our voices, finding the courage to speak up and speak out is an act of bravery. It requires self-assurance, self-belief, and a steadfast commitment to staying true to oneself, even in the face of opposition or adversity.

The Person I Became

Building confidence was a gradual process for me, shaped by various experiences and challenges. As a nurse, I quickly realized that confidence was essential not only for my professional growth but also for the quality of care I provided to my patients. Confidence enabled me to make informed decisions, advocate for my patients, and collaborate successfully with my colleagues. It became evident that a confident voice was a powerful tool in the healthcare environment, driving positive outcomes and fostering trust and respect.

As a clinical nurse instructor, confidence became even more crucial. Lecturing and guiding students in both classroom and clinical settings required me to project confidence in my knowledge and teaching abilities. My students looked to me for information, inspiration, and reassurance. By demonstrating confidence, I created a supportive learning environment where students felt empowered to ask questions, take risks, and grow in their practice. This confidence was not about having all the answers but about being secure in my expertise and willing to engage in the learning process alongside my students.

Confidence also played a significant role in my personal life, especially in teaching my children the importance of effective communication and standing up for themselves. In today's world, where bullying and peer pressure are prevalent, children must develop the confidence to speak up and advocate for themselves. I made it a priority to model this behavior for my kids, demonstrating through my actions and words how to handle difficult situations with courage and self-assurance. By fostering an environment where their voices were heard and valued, I aimed to equip them with the tools they needed to navigate challenges.

Moreover, I sought to instill in my children that confidence is not about being loud or forceful but about firmly believing in one's worth and abilities. Effective communication, whether in personal or professional contexts, stems from this inner confidence. Teaching my kids to articulate their thoughts, express their needs, and assert their boundaries was crucial to their development. I wanted them to know that their voices mattered and that they had the right to be heard and respected.

The importance of confidence has broader implications for community and societal change. When people are confident in their ability to speak up about issues that matter to them, they can drive meaningful conversations and advocate for positive change. This is particularly relevant in professional settings, where confident voices can challenge the status quo, promote innovation, and foster a culture of continuous improvement.

The Person I Became

In my professional journey, I have consistently recognized and acted upon the need to address and mitigate bullying within the nursing profession. The pervasive notion that "nurses eat their young"—a phrase suggesting that experienced nurses often bully new nurses—was something I could not tolerate. Ensuring a supportive and nurturing environment for novice nurses became one of my core missions.

From the outset of my career, I quickly realized the detrimental impact of bullying on new nurses. It undermined their confidence and affected their performance and, ultimately, patient care. This awareness fueled my commitment to speaking out against bullying and advocating for a workplace culture of respect and support.

One of the first steps I took was to establish open channels of communication where new nurses could voice their concerns without fear of retribution. I encouraged them to share their experiences and created a safe space for these discussions. By listening to their stories, I gained valuable insights into their challenges and areas where intervention was most needed.

Additionally, I actively spoke out against bullying behaviors whenever I encountered them. Whether in meetings, during rounds, or in one-on-one conversations, I made it clear that such behavior was unacceptable. I emphasized the importance of professionalism, respect, and teamwork. My goal was to foster an environment where everyone felt valued and supported regardless of their experience level.

Understanding that empowerment comes through knowledge, I provided new nurses with resources and training to help them navigate their roles confidently. This included workshops on effective communication, conflict resolution, and assertiveness. I also paired them with experienced mentors who exemplified positive and supportive behavior. These mentors were role models and offered guidance, helping new nurses build their confidence and professional skills.

One of the most rewarding aspects of this advocacy was witnessing the transformation among the novice nurses. With the right support and encouragement, they began to find their voices, stand up for themselves, and contribute more actively to the team. Their growing confidence and competence led to improved patient outcomes and a cohesive work environment.

Furthermore, by addressing bullying and promoting a culture of respect, we improved the immediate work environment and set a precedent for other departments and institutions to follow. The ripple effect of this change was profound, underscoring the broader implications of confident voices in driving societal change.

In addition to my efforts within the nursing team, I advocated for organizational policies that supported anti-bullying initiatives. This included collaborating with hospital administration to implement training programs and establish clear protocols for reporting and addressing bullying incidents. Institutionalizing these measures ensured that the commitment to a respectful and supportive work environment was upheld at all levels.

My experiences advocating for novice nurses and speaking out against bullying have reinforced my belief in the power of a confident voice. I have seen firsthand that when we have the courage to speak out, we can effect meaningful change that benefits individuals and entire communities. This advocacy work has not only supported new nurses but has also strengthened my resolve to continue using my voice for positive change.

Reflecting on my journey, I realize that confidence in one's voice is a dynamic and evolving quality. It grows with experience, practice, and self-reflection. It involves overcoming self-doubt and pushing through fear, understanding that each step taken in confidence builds a stronger foundation for future challenges.

Whether stepping into new roles, advocating for myself and others, or guiding the next generation of nurses and my own children, confidence has been a cornerstone of my personal and professional development.

But confidence alone is not enough—it's also essential to cultivate a positive mindset and a sense of empowerment that allows us to embrace our voice with courage. This involves recognizing the inherent worth and value of our own experiences and trusting in the power of our voice to effect positive. It's about understanding that our voice has the ability to shape hearts and minds, challenge assumptions, and inspire action for the greater good.

Another important aspect of the power of voice is the ability to be approachable while also setting boundaries. Finding this balance is crucial for maintaining healthy relationships and effective communication. It means being open and receptive to others' perspectives while honoring our own needs and priorities. This involves listening with empathy and understanding, standing firm in our convictions and values, and creating a space for dialogue and collaboration where diverse voices are heard and respected. Such an environment allows meaningful change to take root and flourish.

In today's world, where diversity, equity, and inclusion (DEI) are increasingly prominent, ensuring that all voices are heard and included is more important than ever. DEI encompasses practices and policies designed to support individuals from various backgrounds and provide them with the resources they need to thrive in the workplace. A DEI framework considers factors such as race, gender, and sexual orientation, enabling teams to support employees from marginalized groups effectively.

In my professional and personal life, I have always strived to be approachable while maintaining clear boundaries. This balance fosters trust and respect, encouraging open communication and collaboration. Being approachable means making yourself available to listen, showing empathy, and validating others' experiences. At the same time, it requires setting limits to protect your time, energy, and well-being.

When colleagues, mentees, or students come to me with their concerns or ideas, I make it a point to listen actively and without judgment. This approach helps build rapport and demonstrates that I value their input. However, being approachable doesn't mean agreeing with everything or sacrificing your principles. It's about creating a space where diverse perspectives can be shared and considered.

One practical way to ensure all voices are heard is by fostering an inclusive environment where everyone feels safe to express their opinions. This involves setting ground rules for respectful communication and actively inviting contributions from all team members, especially those who might feel marginalized or overlooked. In meetings, I make it a point to encourage participation from quieter members and acknowledge the value of their contributions. This inclusive approach not only enriches the discussion but also empowers individuals to share their unique perspectives.

Incorporating a DEI framework into our daily interactions is crucial for creating an inclusive environment. This involves recognizing and addressing the unique challenges faced by individuals from diverse backgrounds, such as understanding the systemic barriers that marginalized groups often encounter and actively working to dismantle these obstacles. By doing so, we foster a more equitable environment where everyone has the opportunity to succeed.

Setting boundaries is equally important for maintaining healthy relationships. Clear boundaries help prevent burnout and ensure that interactions remain respectful and productive. For instance, when mentoring, I establish specific meeting times and define the scope of my support. This approach manages expectations and ensures that our time together is focused and effective. Boundaries also protect my well-being, allowing me to offer my best to those I mentor without compromising my own needs.

Balancing approachability with boundary-setting also involves standing firm in our convictions and values. While it is essential to be open to other's perspectives, it is equally important to remain true to our principles. This may involve respectfully disagreeing with someone or taking a stand on issues that matter deeply. By doing so, we model integrity and demonstrate that it is possible to be both open and principled.

This balance is particularly significant in the context of DEI. Advocating for DEI means being a vocal ally for marginalized groups and challenging practices or behaviors that perpetuate inequality. It involves using our voices to promote policies that support diversity and inclusion while also listening to and amplifying the voices of those directly affected by these issues. By creating an environment where all voices are heard and respected, we pave the way for meaningful and lasting change.

The Person I Became

Balancing approachability with boundary-setting has been crucial in my professional journey, especially in mentorship and education. Working with mentees and students requires a delicate equilibrium between being supportive and maintaining professional standards. I achieve this balance by establishing clear expectations and boundaries from the start. During our initial meetings, I outline objectives, expected outcomes, and methods of evaluation. This process helps create a foundation of mutual respect and aligns our goals.

Setting boundaries does not mean being rigid or unapproachable. Instead, it involves creating a framework within which productive and respectful interactions can occur. By clearly defining the scope of our interactions, mentees and students understand the limits and expectations, which helps prevent misunderstandings and ensures that our time together is focused and effective. This approach fosters a positive learning environment where everyone feels valued and respected.

For example, I emphasize balancing their availability and personal and professional responsibilities when mentoring new nurse educators. I encourage them to be open to questions and discussions and designate specific times for these interactions to prevent burnout. By modeling this behavior, I demonstrate that it is possible to be approachable while maintaining necessary boundaries.

Listening with empathy and understanding is another crucial aspect of this balance. When mentees or students approach me with concerns or questions, I strive to listen actively and without judgment. This approach helps build trust and rapport, making them feel comfortable sharing their thoughts and challenges. However, while I am open to their perspectives, I also ensure that my own values and professional standards are upheld. This might involve guiding them toward finding solutions or reinforcing certain non-negotiable principles and practices.

Creating a space for dialogue and collaboration is essential for fostering an inclusive and respectful environment. In my experience, facilitating group discussions where everyone has the opportunity to contribute helps cultivate a sense of community and shared purpose. This collaborative approach enhances learning and empowers individuals to take ownership of their growth and development.

Moreover, being approachable and setting boundaries extends beyond professional interactions to personal relationships. In my family life, I strive to be open and present for my children, listening to their concerns and supporting their endeavors. At the same time, I set boundaries to ensure that my needs and priorities are also respected. This balance is crucial for maintaining harmony and mutual respect within our household.

In addition to being approachable, it's crucial to set boundaries and assert ourselves when necessary. This involves knowing when to speak up, when to step back, and how to balance our own needs and priorities while advocating for ourselves and others. Recognizing that our voice is a precious gift—one that deserves to be honored, respected, and protected—is essential.

Ultimately, the power of voice lies in embracing our unique perspective, voice, and storytelling to connect with others on a deep and meaningful level. It's about having the courage to speak our truth, share our experiences, and use our voices to effect positive change in the world. By embracing our voice with confidence, authenticity, and conviction, we can inspire, empower, and make a difference in the lives of others.

As I reflect on the power of my own voice, I am reminded of Maya Angelou's words: "Your voice is a reflection of your character, your strength, and your values. Use it wisely, use it boldly, and use it to make a difference in the world." May we all find the courage to embrace our voices with confidence and conviction, knowing that with the power of our voices, anything is possible. As I continue my journey, I am grateful for the power and influence of my voice, and I urge you to reflect on the power of your voice.

Chapter 7:
Embrace Experiences, Emotions, and Viewpoints

Life is a woven masterpiece with many experiences, emotions, and viewpoints—a rich fabric that shapes our perspectives, attitudes, and understanding of the world. In the journey of self-discovery and personal growth, embracing these elements is essential for deepening our self-awareness, cultivating empathy for others, and fostering a sense of connection and belonging.

Embracing Experiences

One of the most profound lessons I've learned about embracing experiences is the importance of living with an open heart and an adventurous spirit. Every experience—whether joyful or challenging, mundane, or extraordinary—offers an opportunity for growth, learning, and self-discovery. By approaching new experiences with curiosity, courage, and an open mind, we expand our horizons, broaden our perspectives, and enrich our lives in ways we never imagined.

1. The Adventure of New Experiences

Living with an adventurous spirit doesn't necessarily mean seeking out extreme activities or constantly pushing boundaries. Instead, it involves approaching each day with a sense of wonder and a willingness to step outside our comfort zones. This can be as simple as trying a new cuisine, traveling to a new place, or learning a new skill. Every new experience offers the potential for personal growth and a deeper understanding of ourselves and the world.

When we think of adventure, we might picture skydiving, mountain climbing, or exploring remote jungles. While these activities are certainly adventurous, the essence of adventure lies not in the extremity of the activity but in the mindset we bring to it. Adventure is about curiosity—seeing the world with fresh eyes and being open to what it has to offer. It's about saying yes to opportunities that come our way and creating our own when none seem present.

Consider the transformative power of travel. Visiting new places, whether near or far, exposes us to different cultures, languages, and ways of life. It challenges our preconceptions and broadens our understanding of humanity. Every journey, even a short trip to a neighboring town, can become an adventure if approached with curiosity and openness.

2. Finding Meaning in Everyday Moments

Embracing experiences is not just about seeking out new adventures; it's also about finding meaning and purpose in the everyday moments of life. From the simple joys of a quiet morning walk to the lessons learned from overcoming obstacles, every experience can teach us something new about ourselves, others, and the world around us. By cultivating mindfulness and presence in each moment, we can find beauty, wonder, and inspiration in the ordinary.

I've made it a habit to start my mornings with deep breathing and relaxation, avoiding the temptation to check my phone or social media. These distractions only consume valuable time and pull me away from my focus. Instead, I dedicate my first moments to meditating and planning for the day ahead with an overview of the task list I had created the night before. This simple practice allows me to approach the day with clarity and purpose, keeping me grounded and better prepared for whatever comes my way. Along with deep breathing, I've found that a light morning stretch can further enhance relaxation and boost energy. Staying hydrated by drinking a glass of water upon waking helps jumpstart my metabolism and sets a healthy tone for the day.

When approached mindfully, mundane tasks we often overlook or take for granted can become sources of joy and meaning. For example, preparing a meal can transform into a meditative practice when done with intention and presence. This daily activity connects us to the ingredients we use, the traditions they represent, and the people with whom we share our food.

Similarly, daily rituals such as drinking coffee in the morning become moments of reflection and gratitude. I cultivate a deeper appreciation for life's simple pleasures by savoring these small moments. Walking in nature or watching the changing colors of the sky at sunset reminds us of the beauty and interconnectedness of the natural world.

Another part of my daily routine that brings me peace is stopping at the Waterview on my way to or from work. There's something profoundly calming about the sight of the water and the changing skies above. I often take a moment to pause, breathe in the fresh air, and capture the scene in photographs. In these quiet moments of connection with nature, I find a sense of tranquility, a reminder to slow down and appreciate the beauty around me. These experiences, though seemingly ordinary, hold profound meaning when approached with mindfulness and gratitude.

3. The Power of Reflection

Reflection is a critical component of embracing experiences. Reflecting on our experiences allows us to gain valuable insights into our thoughts, behaviors, and emotions. This reflection can take many forms, from journaling to meditation, enabling us to process our experiences, learn from them, and integrate those lessons into our lives. Journaling encourages us to slow down and articulate our emotions, leading to greater self-awareness and clarity. Journaling allowed me to create a space to explore my inner world and make sense of my experiences. Writing about my thoughts and feelings helped me uncover patterns, identify areas for growth, and celebrate the little achievements.

Reflecting on our experiences also involves seeking feedback from others. Open and honest conversations with trusted friends, family members, or mentors can offer new perspectives and insights. By listening to others' viewpoints and being receptive to constructive criticism, we deepen our understanding and grow from our experiences.

Conversely, meditation lets us quiet our minds and observe our thoughts without judgment. Through regular meditation practice, we develop greater mindfulness and presence, enabling us to respond to experiences with equanimity and compassion.

Embracing Emotions

In addition to embracing experiences, it's crucial to embrace our emotions—the full spectrum of human feelings that enrich our lives and deepen our connections with others. From joy and love to sadness and grief, and from anger and frustration to gratitude and awe, our emotions are a powerful force that guides, motivates, and helps us navigate life's complexities. By embracing our emotions with compassion and acceptance, we cultivate emotional resilience, strengthen our relationships, and live with greater authenticity and integrity.

1. Understanding Emotional Resilience

Emotional resilience is the ability to adapt to stressful situations and cope with life's challenges. By embracing our emotions, we can develop this resilience, enabling us to recover more quickly from setbacks and maintain a positive outlook even in difficult times.

Emotional resilience involves a blend of self-awareness, self-regulation, and social support. Self-awareness helps us recognize and understand our emotions, while self-regulation enables us to manage our responses constructively. Social support, whether from friends, family, or professional counselors, provides a network of care and understanding that strengthens our resilience.

Building emotional resilience requires a proactive approach to emotional health. Practices such as mindfulness meditation, regular physical exercise, and a balanced lifestyle are crucial for our overall well-being and enhance our ability to cope with stress. Mindfulness meditation trains us to observe our thoughts and emotions without judgment, enabling us to respond to challenges with greater clarity and calm.

2. The Role of Vulnerability

But embracing emotions is not always easy—it requires vulnerability, courage, and a willingness to lean into discomfort. It means allowing ourselves to feel deeply, acknowledge our vulnerabilities, and express ourselves authentically, even when uncomfortable or challenging. By embracing our emotions with openness and compassion, we can cultivate a deeper sense of self-awareness, self-compassion, and emotional well-being, empowering us to live with greater authenticity. Vulnerability is often seen as a weakness, but it is actually a source of strength. When we allow ourselves to be vulnerable, we open ourselves to deeper connections with others and more profound personal growth. Vulnerability involves sharing our true selves with those we trust. This openness fosters intimacy and trust in our relationships, creating a supportive environment where we can thrive.

The willingness to lean into discomfort is a key aspect of embracing vulnerability. Life is full of uncertainties and challenges, and avoiding discomfort only limits our growth and potential. By facing our fears and embracing the unknown, we build resilience and expand our capacity for joy and fulfillment. This process requires courage and a commitment to personal growth, but the rewards are immeasurable.

3. The Importance of Emotional Expression

Expressing our emotions is essential for both our mental and emotional well-being. Whether it's talking with a friend, engaging in creative activities, or seeking professional support, this process allows us to navigate and release our feelings. Moreover, expressing our emotions deepens our connections with others. It gives us the opportunity to share our authentic selves, fostering relationships built on trust and mutual understanding.

Creative outlets such as art, music, writing, and dance offer powerful avenues for emotional expression. These activities allow us to channel our emotions into tangible forms, providing a sense of release and catharsis. Engaging in creative expression not only enhances our self-awareness but also helps us process complex feelings that may be difficult to articulate in words.

Talking with trusted friends or family members offers another valuable means of emotional expression. These conversations create opportunities for mutual support and understanding, strengthening our relationships and fostering a sense of belonging. Additionally, seeking professional support from therapists or counselors can provide essential tools and strategies for managing emotions and navigating life's challenges.

Embracing Viewpoints

Embracing diverse viewpoints means recognizing the richness of human experience and honoring the perspectives of others with empathy, respect, and understanding. In an increasingly polarized world, this approach is vital for fostering meaningful dialogue, promoting inclusivity, and building bridges of understanding and compassion across divides. By approaching differing viewpoints with openness and curiosity, we can cultivate empathy, strengthen connections, and contribute to a more compassionate and inclusive world for all.

1. The Value of Diverse Perspectives

Everyone brings a unique perspective shaped by their experiences, culture, and background. Embracing diverse viewpoints enriches our understanding of the world and challenges our assumptions. It encourages critical thinking and invites us to consider different angles, fostering a more comprehensive and nuanced outlook.

In our increasingly globalized world, exposure to diverse perspectives is more accessible than ever. Through literature, art, media, and personal interactions, we have countless opportunities to learn from people with varying cultural backgrounds, beliefs, and experiences. Engaging with these perspectives broadens our horizons and deepens our empathy.

Diverse perspectives also stimulate innovation and creativity. When we bring together individuals with different viewpoints and backgrounds, we create fertile ground for new ideas and solutions. This diversity of thought enhances problem-solving and drives progress across various fields, from science and technology to social and cultural initiatives.

2. Fostering Meaningful Dialogue

Engaging in meaningful dialogue with others who hold different viewpoints can be challenging but rewarding. It requires active listening, open-mindedness, and a willingness to engage in respectful debate. Such dialogue fosters greater understanding and cooperation, helping to bridge divides and build a more inclusive society.

Active listening is a fundamental skill for meaningful dialogue. It involves fully focusing on the speaker, acknowledging their points, and responding thoughtfully. Active listening not only shows respect for the other person's perspective but also creates a safe space for open communication.

Open-mindedness is another crucial aspect of meaningful dialogue. It means being willing to consider and understand viewpoints different from our own, even if we ultimately disagree with them. Open-mindedness fosters mutual respect and encourages the exchange of ideas.

Respectful debate is essential for navigating differences and finding common ground. It involves presenting our views clearly and calmly, without resorting to personal attacks or dismissive language.

3. Building Empathy and Connection

We build stronger connections with others by embracing viewpoints with empathy and respect. This involves recognizing the common humanity that underlies our differences and approaching conversations with a genuine desire to understand and learn from others. In doing so, we create a compassionate and connected world.

Empathy is the ability to understand and share another's feelings. It involves putting ourselves in someone else's shoes and seeing the world from their perspective. Practicing empathy allows us to connect on a deeper level and fosters a sense of solidarity and compassion. Building empathy involves listening to others' stories, asking questions, and striving to understand their experiences and emotions. It also means reflecting on our own biases and assumptions and being open to changing our perspectives based on what we learn. The connection stems from empathy and mutual understanding. When we connect with others, we create bonds of trust and support that enrich our lives and foster a sense of community. These connections are vital for our well-being and for building a more inclusive and compassionate society.

The Journey of Embracing Life

As I reflect on my journey of embracing experiences, emotions, and viewpoints, I am reminded of the poet Mary Oliver's words: "Tell me, what is it you plan to do with your one wild and precious life?" Each experience, each emotion, each viewpoint is a precious gift—a chance to learn, grow, and connect with the world in meaningful and profound ways. By approaching life with an open heart and a willingness to learn, we can cultivate a life filled with joy, meaning, and purpose, and create a world that reflects the beauty and diversity of the human experience.

Embracing life fully involves seeking out joy and meaning in every moment. It means being present, appreciating the small things, and finding gratitude even in challenging times. By living with intention and purpose, we can create a life that is rich, fulfilling, and aligned with our values. Cultivating joy involves discovering and nurturing activities and relationships that bring us happiness and fulfillment. This might include hobbies, creative pursuits, spending time with loved ones, or engaging in acts of kindness. By prioritizing these sources of joy, we lay a positive foundation for our lives.

Finding meaning involves identifying what is most important to us and aligning our actions with our values and goals. This might include pursuing a career that aligns with our passions, volunteering for causes we care about, or engaging in practices that promote personal growth and well-being. Living with meaning provides us with a sense of purpose and direction.

The Impact on Personal Growth

This journey of embracing experiences, emotions, and viewpoints is a continuous process of personal growth. It challenges us to evolve, become more self-aware, and develop a deeper understanding of ourselves and others. Though this growth is not always easy, it is profoundly rewarding.

The impact of personal growth extends beyond ourselves. As we grow and evolve, we become more capable of contributing to the well-being of others and making a positive impact on the world. Personal growth enhances our ability to lead, inspire, and create meaningful change in our communities.

Our individual actions, though seemingly small, have a ripple effect that can create broader social change. By embracing our own experiences, emotions, and viewpoints with openness and empathy, we set an example for others and contribute to a culture of compassion and understanding.

In conclusion, embracing experiences, emotions, and viewpoints is a powerful practice that can transform our lives and the world around us. It encourages us to live with courage, curiosity, and compassion, and to approach each day with an open heart and mind. By doing so, we create a life that is vibrant, meaningful, and deeply connected to the rich tapestry of human experience.

The Person I Became

As I reflect on my journey of embracing experiences, emotions, and viewpoints, I am reminded of the opportunities to learn, grow, and connect with the world around us in meaningful and profound ways. I encourage you to reflect and embrace these experiences in your own journey.

Conclusion: Embrace Your Journey

As we come to the end of this journey together, I am filled with gratitude for the opportunity to share my story, experiences, and insights with you with the purpose to uplift and encourage. Throughout this book, we have explored the many facets of personal growth, resilience, and authenticity—universal and timeless themes that are deeply personal and unique to everyone's journey.

Throughout these pages, we have delved into the importance of staying true to oneself and embracing authenticity with courage and conviction. We have explored the power of mentorship, connection, and community in shaping our paths and supporting us along the way. We have celebrated the transformative power of positivity and personal development and embraced our unique perspectives, voices, and storytelling to resonate with others on a deep and meaningful level.

We've learned that success is not merely about reaching a destination but about embracing the journey with an open heart and a willingness to grow and evolve along the way. We've discovered that each setback is not a roadblock but a stepping stone on the path to success. And we've recognized that the journey of self-discovery is not just about personal growth but about fostering empathy, understanding, and connection with those around us.

As we reflect on the key themes and messages of this book, one overarching theme emerges—empowerment. Empowerment to embrace our true selves, to follow our passions and dreams, and to live with courage, resilience, and authenticity. Empowerment to overcome obstacles, navigate challenges, and embrace change with grace and confidence. And empowerment to make a positive impact in the world, to build movements that inspire, empower, and unite people from all walks of life in pursuit of a common vision for a better, more just world.

As you embark on your own journey of growth and authenticity, I leave you with this final message of empowerment and encouragement. Embrace your journey with an open heart and a willingness to learn, grow, and evolve along the way. Trust in your strength, resilience, and inner wisdom to guide you through life's challenges and triumphs. And above all, remember that you have the power to shape your destiny, create a life filled with passion and purpose, and make a positive impact in the world in your own unique way.

The Person I Became

As you embrace your journey with courage, resilience, and authenticity, may you find joy, meaning, and fulfillment in every moment. May you continue to inspire, empower, and uplift those around you with your unique perspective, voice, and storytelling. By embracing your journey with an open heart and a willingness to grow, you have the power to create a future that reflects the beauty and diversity of the human experience and to make a lasting impact on the world that will be felt for generations to come.

Congratulations on completing *The Person I Became*. May your journey continue with passion, purpose, and empowerment. Thank you for joining me on this path of growth and authenticity. May your path be filled with light, love, and endless possibilities.

Appendix:
Resources for Continued Growth

In this appendix, I've compiled a list of resources to support you on your growth, authenticity, and personal development journey. This collection includes books, websites, podcasts, and organizations that offer valuable insights, inspiration, and guidance for navigating life's challenges and embracing your true self. Whether you're seeking practical advice, personal stories, or spiritual wisdom, these resources are here to aid you in your journey of self-discovery and empowerment.

Books
- **"The Power of Now"** by Eckhart Tolle
- **"Daring Greatly: How the Courage to Be Vulnerable Transforms the Way We Live, Love, Parent, and Lead"** by Brené Brown
- **"Mindset: The New Psychology of Success"** by Carol S. Dweck
- **"The Gifts of Imperfection: Let Go of Who You Think You're Supposed to Be and Embrace Who You Are"** by Brené Brown
- **"Man's Search for Meaning"** by Viktor E. Frankl

- "You Are a Badass: How to Stop Doubting Your Greatness and Start Living an Awesome Life" by Jen Sincero
- "Big Magic: Creative Living Beyond Fear" by Elizabeth Gilbert
- "The Four Agreements: A Practical Guide to Personal Freedom" by Don Miguel Ruiz
- "Atomic Habits: An Easy & Proven Way to Build Good Habits & Break Bad Ones" by James Clear
- "The Subtle Art of Not Giving a F*ck: A Counterintuitive Approach to Living a Good Life" by Mark Manson
- "Total Money Makeover" by Dave Ramsey
- "Rich Dad Poor Dad" by Robert Kiyosaki
- "Juggling Elephants: An Easier Way to Get Your Most Important Things Done--Now!" by Jones Loflin and Todd Musig
- "Resilience" by Sandra Adom

Websites and Blogs
- **Tiny Buddha** (tinybuddha.com)
- **Psychology Today** (psychologytoday.com)
- **Greater Good Magazine** (greatergood.berkeley.edu)
- **TED Talks** (ted.com)
- **Mindful** (mindful.org)

- **Zen Habits** (zenhabits.net)
- **The Minimalists** (theminimalists.com)
- **Marc and Angel Hack Life** (marcandangel.com)
- **Live Your Legend** (liveyourlegend.net)
- **Oprah.com** (oprah.com)

Podcasts
- **The Tim Ferriss Show**
- **The Tony Robbins Podcast**
- **The School of Greatness with Lewis Howes**
- **On Being with Krista Tippett**
- **The Minimalists Podcast**
- **The Marie Forleo Podcast**
- **The Joe Rogan Experience**
- **Happier with Gretchen Rubin**
- **The Rich Roll Podcast**
- **Unlocking Us with Brené Brown**

Organizations and Communities
- **The American Psychological Association (APA)**
- **The International Coach Federation (ICF)**
- **Mindfulness-Based Stress Reduction (MBSR) Programs**
- **Toastmasters International**

- **The Center for Nonviolent Communication (NVC)**
- **The Chopra Center**
- **The Center for Mindful Self-Compassion**
- **The National Alliance on Mental Illness (NAMI)**
- **The World Happiness Summit (WOHASU)**

Meetup Groups (meetup.com): Search for groups in your area that promote personal development, mindfulness, spirituality, and more.

These resources are just a starting point for your journey of growth and authenticity. Explore, experiment, and find what resonates with you on your path. Remember, the journey of self-discovery is unique to each individual, and there is no one-size-fits-all approach. Trust your intuition, follow your heart, and know that you have the power to create a life filled with purpose, passion, and fulfillment.

Summary

Introduction:
Welcome to *The Person I Became*. I invite you to embark on a journey of personal growth, resilience, and empowerment with me. Within these pages, I'll share my experiences, insights, and the lessons I've learned as I navigated life's twists and turns, all while striving to become the best version of myself.

Chapter 1: Defining the Journey
My journey began with a simple yet profound inspiration: to leave a legacy for my loved ones and empower them through authenticity and openness. Along the way, I faced numerous milestones and challenges that have shaped who I am today. From balancing work, education, and family responsibilities to overcoming financial struggles, each experience has taught me invaluable lessons in resilience and perseverance.

Chapter 2: Balancing Act
Balancing the demands of work, education, and family life was no easy feat. There were moments of doubt and uncertainty, but through it all, I learned the importance of prioritizing self-care and setting boundaries. By embracing my own needs and learning to

say no without guilt, I found the strength to overcome financial obstacles and pursue my dreams with determination.

Chapter 3: Lessons Learned

Through the ups and downs of my journey, I discovered the transformative power of resilience, adaptability, and maintaining a positive outlook. I learned to view change as inevitable and to find the silver lining in every situation. By setting goals and staying focused, I achieved success at a young age—obtaining my nursing degree, starting my own business, and eventually earning a doctorate.

Chapter 4: Guided by Mentorship

Mentorship has played a crucial role in my journey, offering guidance, support, and inspiration when I needed it most. From the personal mentors who believed in me to my own experiences as a mentor, I've witnessed firsthand the profound impact of mentorship on personal and professional growth. By surrounding myself with positive influences and seeking advice with an open mind, I've been able to navigate life's challenges with confidence and resilience.

The Person I Became

Chapter 5: From Struggle to Success

My journey from overcoming financial struggles to achieving academic and professional success has been marked by both challenges and triumphs. As a nurse educator, I've had the privilege of contributing to the nursing field and inspiring the next generation of healthcare professionals. Through it all, I've learned the importance of personal growth, nurturing relationships, and embracing my identity with pride.

Chapter 6: The Power of Voice

Confidence, positivity, and adaptability have been guiding principles throughout my journey, empowering me to speak up, embrace change, and pursue my passions with conviction. By sharing my story authentically and connecting with readers on a deeper level, I hope to inspire others to embrace their own uniqueness and create positive change in their lives and communities.

Chapter 7: Embrace Experiences, Emotions, and Viewpoints

Life is a tapestry woven with a myriad of experiences, emotions, and viewpoints—a rich fabric that shapes our perspectives, attitudes, and understanding of the world. By embracing our

The Person I Became

journey with an open heart and a willingness to learn, grow, and evolve, we uncover the beauty and depth of the human experience.

Conclusion: Embrace Your Journey

As we conclude this journey together, I offer you a final message of empowerment and encouragement. Embrace your path with courage, resilience, and authenticity, knowing you have the power to create a life filled with purpose, passion, and fulfillment. Trust in your strength, resilience, and inner wisdom to guide you through life's challenges and triumphs. Remember, you have the power to shape your own destiny, craft a future that reflects the beauty and diversity of the human experience, and make a lasting impact in the world in your own unique way.

Closing Remarks

As I come to the end of this memoir, I am reminded that the journey of self-discovery and growth is never truly finished. Life continues to unfold in ways that challenge, inspire, and shape us into the people we are meant to become. *The Person I Became* is not the final chapter of my story, but a reflection on the lessons I've learned so far—lessons about vulnerability, resilience, empathy, and the power of embracing every aspect of life.

I hope that as you have read these pages, you have found moments that resonate with your own journey. My story is just one of many, but I believe that we all share a common desire to live authentically, to connect with others, and to find meaning in the experiences that define our lives. If nothing else, I hope this memoir has inspired you to reflect on your own path with an open heart and to embrace the person you are becoming.

As we move forward, may we continue to grow with courage and curiosity. May we find strength in vulnerability, joy in the everyday, and connection in our shared humanity. The person you are becoming is a beautiful, ever-evolving work of art, and I am grateful to have shared a part of that journey with you.

The Person I Became

But this is not the end. Life continues to unfold, and with it, new chapters await. In my next book, I look forward to diving even deeper into the journey complexities of leadership, resilience, and the pursuit of purpose—exploring the lessons I've learned as a healthcare professional and as a person navigating the challenges of an ever-changing world.

Thank you for reading, and may your own journey be filled with discovery, compassion, and purpose.

Made in the USA
Middletown, DE
18 October 2024